Brazil under the Workers' Party

T0161501

Praise for the book

'This book offers a fresh and highly informative introduction to the history, achievements and limitations of the federal administrations led by the Workers' Party (PT) in Brazil. Brazilian society and its economy have been transformed under Luís Inácio Lula da Silva and Dilma Rousseff. However, today the PT model is in crisis. Sue Branford and Jan Rocha explain better than anyone else why this is the case, and why it is important to reconstitute and relaunch the left in Brazil.'

Professor Alfredo Saad-Filho, SOAS,
University of London

'Sue Branford and Jan Rocha, brilliant chroniclers of Brazil's recent history, explain in this alarming and riveting book the popular disenchantment that now faces the Workers' Party, leaving the country vulnerable to the return of the right, and to the possible collapse not just of its left-wing government but of the "pink tide" in Latin America as a whole.'

Richard Gott, author of Hugo Chávez and
the Bolivarian Revolution

'Brazil under the Workers' Party is hugely enlightening, a balanced but critical analysis of a tumultuous period. It manages to give a strong sense of the tendencies, movements, debates and dilemmas, while steering through their detail, to arrive at a sober and sobering appraisal of the PT's record in government.'

David H. Treece, Camoens Professor of
Portuguese, Kings College London

'Sue Branford and Jan Rocha's gutsy new book provides a succinct yet thoughtful contribution to a growing debate over Brazil's Workers' Party and its experience at the helm of four national governments since 2003. Two seasoned journalists, who know Brazil inside out, tell an effective story. Their tale, above all, captures the climate of angst, uncertainty and frustration among the Brazilian left, as President Dilma Rousseff enters her second term in office.'

Miguel Carter, Founding Director, DEMOS –
Centro para la Democracia, la
Creatividad y la Inclusión Social, Asunción

'Branford and Rocha are amongst the most careful, committed and insightful analysts of Brazil and have followed the history of the PT from its origins. What they write here is of immense importance. They show that there is much to learn from the ambivalent and disappointing fate of a world-changing historical project. I recommend this book enthusiastically and strongly.'

Hilary Wainwright, founding editor Red Pepper,
Fellow of the Transnational Institute and
writer on radical political parties and
experiments in political transformation

'Branford and Rocha's thoughtful study of the rise and fall of the Workers' Party in Brazil should be required reading for all those seeking to understand the crisis facing social democratic parties the world over. The party's rejection of agrarian reform, tax justice or structural political change lost it the support of Brazil's powerful social movements, while its recent adoption of classic austerity policies has forfeited its very legitimacy. The authors' conclusion is a compelling one: for left parties, transformative social and political change is the only hope of success.'

John Hilary, Executive Director, War on
Want, author of The Poverty of Capitalism

'This book is lively, imaginative and provocative. Not everyone will agree with its critique of recent PT governments, but it will spark debate about the recent political history and possible futures of Brazil.'

Professor Anthony Pereira, Director,
King's Brazil Institute, King's College London

Brazil under the Workers' Party

From euphoria to despair

Sue Branford and Jan Rocha

PRACTICAL ACTION
Publishing

Practical Action Publishing Ltd
The Schumacher Centre,
Bourton on Dunsmore, Rugby,
Warwickshire, CV23 9QZ, UK
www.practicalactionpublishing.org

A catalogue record for this book is available from the British Library.

A catalogue record for this book has been requested from the Library of Congress.

ISBN 9781909014008 Hardback
ISBN 9781909014015 Paperback
ISBN 9781909013902 Library Ebook
ISBN 9781909013896 Ebook

Citation: Branford, S., and Rocha, J., (2015) *Brazil Under the Workers' Party: from euphoria to despair*, Rugby, UK: Practical Action Publishing, <http://dx.doi.org/10.3362/9781909013902>

Since 1974, Practical Action Publishing has published and disseminated books and information in support of international development work throughout the world. Practical Action Publishing is a trading name of Practical Action Publishing Ltd (Company Reg. No. 1159018), the wholly owned publishing company of Practical Action. Practical Action Publishing trades only in support of its parent charity objectives and any profits are covenanted back to Practical Action (Charity Reg. No. 247257, Group VAT Registration No. 880 9924 76).

The views and opinions in this publication are those of the author and do not represent those of Practical Action Publishing Ltd or its parent charity Practical Action. Reasonable efforts have been made to publish reliable data and information, but the authors and publisher cannot assume responsibility for the validity of all materials or for the consequences of their use.

Cover design by Andrew Corbett
Typeset by Allzone Digital
Printed in the United Kingdom

Contents

http://dx.doi.org/10.3362/9781909013902.000

Introduction

When Dilma Rousseff strode up the ramp to the presidential palace on 1 January 2015, it marked the fourth consecutive time that a candidate from the PT (Partido dos Trabalhadores, Workers' Party) *had taken office. The country had narrowly, yet decisively, backed continuation of the PT's programme of change. Or so it seemed. Less than three months later, the country was in turmoil, with hundreds of thousands on the streets in anti-PT demonstrations and calls for Dilma to be impeached. The right was in the ascendancy. What had gone wrong?*

On Sunday March 15 2015 more than half a million Brazilians took to the streets to protest against corruption and to demand the impeachment of President Dilma Rousseff, who only six months earlier had won a tightly-contested roller coaster of an election. Although few of the protesters came from the poorest classes or the trade unions, there was no denying the scale and breadth of the marches. What a contrast with October 2002, when hundreds of thousands celebrated the victory of the PT's charismatic candidate, Luiz Inácio Lula da Silva, an industrial worker. Back then people were waving red flags and some, men and women, were weeping with joy – and disbelief that the left had finally taken power. But in March 2015 the protesters were carrying placards demanding 'Fora Dilma!' (Dilma Out!). One poster read: 'Nation + Liberty = PT Out!' After 12 years of government by the PT (*Partido dos Trabalhadores*, Workers' Party), the right was once again calling the shots.

Signs that all was not well for the PT were evident almost two years earlier in June 2013, when hundreds

http://dx.doi.org/10.3362/9781909013902.001

of thousands took to the streets. Although those protests did not specifically target the government, they expressed widespread dissatisfaction with public services and unhappiness with the reports of widespread corruption. At the time it seemed that the authorities were listening to the voices from the street, but little changed.

Since then, the government has been virtually paralysed, creating a political vacuum into which the right has stepped. President Rousseff's victory in the October 2014 elections was a blip in the process, reflecting the continued strength of the social movements and their reluctance to relinquish their hope that the PT would fashion a new and much more egalitarian Brazil, where the political and economic power of the established elites would be effectively challenged.

But those dreams have now come crashing down. Today there remains little doubt that the left has suffered a huge setback and, unless they can rediscover their sense of purpose, this could turn into a devastating defeat. The full implications of this are only just becoming apparent.

The present climate of despair should not blind one to the PT's considerable achievements. By the end of 2014, President Lula in his two terms and President Rousseff in her first had pulled off two major achievements: they had established Brazil as a regional superpower, with an agenda markedly different from that of the USA; and they had prevented the Brazilian state from having its priorities dictated by multinational corporations, showing that it is still possible to carry out policies that benefit the poor and the excluded (Santos, 2014). Other countries in South America are seeking in different ways to break away from US dominance and to tame corporate capitalism – Venezuela, Argentina, Uruguay, Bolivia, Ecuador and Chile – but Brazil is, by far, the largest and the most influential.

Although this was obscured during the hurly-burly of the dirty electoral campaign, if Dilma had lost, Brazil would already be heading for a very different future. Her rival in the second round, Aécio Neves, wanted to bring Brazil back into the US fold. He would have taken the country out of Mercosul, South America's own trade bloc, and re-opened discussions with the US for the creation of the Free Trade Area of the Americas (FTAA) (Lima, 2014). Had he won, Brazil and probably much of South America would have been subsumed into an expanded North America Free Trade Agreement (NAFTA) where the terms of trade are dictated in the main by US state and corporate interests. The US dream of asserting hegemony over the whole of the Americas would have been revitalized.

The election was very close. Dilma squeaked home in the second round, held on 26 October 2014, receiving 3.5 million votes more than Aécio, out of a total of 107 million, with 30 million abstentions. It was only at the eleventh hour that the social movements went out onto the streets to campaign for Dilma, many of them very reluctantly. 'We voted for her because we realised that a victory for the opposition would be a huge setback', said Natália Szermeta, co-ordinator of the MTST (*Movimento dos Trabalhadores Sem-Teto,* Homeless Workers' Movement) (Senra, 2014).

Why were the social movements so unwilling to endorse Dilma, given that she was the candidate for the Workers' Party (PT) which had already brought such significant change through its social policies? Does this lack of enthusiasm mean that, after 12 years in government, the PT has lost much of its social base?

The evolution of the PT

Brazil's Workers' Party, the *Partido dos Trabalhadores* or PT, emerged in the wake of a series of major strikes in the late 1970s. These mortally wounded the military dictatorship, which was then given the coup de grâce by huge nationwide mobilizations in 1983 and 1984 (Branford and Kucinski, 2003). The Workers' Party attracted traditionally incompatible groups, including Trotskyists, Leninists, Marxists, Catholics from the liberation wing of the Catholic Church, scarcely literate workers and renowned intellectuals. It was the first mass party in Brazil with predominantly socialist ideas and the only mainstream party with activists and political activity outside electoral periods. The objective was to gain power through a combination of mass mobilization and electoral success, and then to transform the social and political structures so that Brazil would become a country of social equality and social justice.

With the return to civilian rule, the party grew fast, winning elections first at the municipal and then at state level (see Tables 1 and 2). But, even though the party had the country's most charismatic leader in Luiz Inácio Lula da Silva, a union leader and former industrial worker, it found it tantalizingly difficult to gain the final prize – the presidency.

For many years the closest Lula came to winning was his first attempt, in 1989. At the time popular enthusiasm for him was huge: large rallies were held around the country and well-known singers participated in the music video, used during the free TV slots, which featured one of the most effective political jingles ever thought up, 'Lula Lá'. However, most of the media lined up behind Lula's opponent Fernando Collor de Mello, a member of the ruling elite, and were determined by

Table 1 Number of PT candidates elected in municipal elections

Year	Mayors	Councillors
1982	2	127
1988	37	1,006
1992	54	1,100
1996	115	1,895
2000	174	2,475

Source: Sue Branford and Bernardo Kucinski, 'Politics transformed: Lula and the Workers' Party in Brazil', Latin America Bureau, London, 2003.

Table 2 Number of PT candidates elected in state elections

Year	PT governors	PT state deputies
1982	0	12
1986	0	40
1990	0	81
1994	2	92
1998	3	90
2002	3	147

Source: Sue Branford and Bernardo Kucinski, 'Politics transformed: Lula and the Workers' Party in Brazil', Latin America Bureau, London, 2003.

fair means or foul to ensure that Lula was not elected. TV Globo, at the height of its dominance, staged a live debate between the two candidates and on the following day aired an edited version of the debate that showed Collor's best moments and Lula's worst. This and other similar attempts to manipulate public opinion may well have determined the outcome of the election. It was not the industrial worker, who had sold peanuts on the streets as a child, but Fernando Collor de Mello, the son of a senator and friend of the owner of TV Globo, who became Brazil's first democratically elected president for 29 years.

Lula ran again, unsuccessfully, in 1994 and 1998. He became frustrated and, according to a close aide, fearful of becoming forever the 'also ran'. He decided it was time to change strategy and said he would only stand for the presidency for a fourth time in 2002 if he were given a free hand to run the campaign in his own way and to make whatever alliances he wanted. This was clearly a blow to the party's internal democracy but, such was its thirst for power, Lula got his way.

He set up a modern press office and hired the country's leading expert in political public relations, even though he was not a member of the PT or even sympathetic towards it. Lula's pragmatic approach paid off and he won the election comfortably with over 60% of the vote (see Table 3).

Some analysts believe that the party paid a heavy price. The history lecturer Valerio Acary says that the

Table 3 Share of the Presidential Vote for PT Candidates Luiz Inácio Lula da Silva and Dilma Rousseff, 1989–2014

Year	Candidate	Number of votes (millions)	Percent of total votes
1989	Lula	31.1	44.2
1994	Lula	17.1	27.0
1998	Lula	21.5	31.2
2002	Lula	52.8	61.3
2006	Lula	58.3	60.8
2010	Dilma	55.8	56.0
2014	Dilma	54.5	51.6

Source: http://pt.wikipedia.org/wiki/Partido_dos_Trabalhadores

PT lost its political edge and became, like so many other political parties in Brazil, a machine for promoting its leader: 'The transformation of *petismo* into *lulismo*, the personality cult of the great leader, had consequences, with the devaluing of collective and independent organisations, like the trade unions and social movements (Acary, 2014).'

Coalition politics

Winning the election was only half the battle; another huge challenge faced the party when it tackled the tricky problem of how it was going to govern. Until 2003 the PT controlled less than 12% of the seats in the Chamber of Deputies. During Lula's two terms as President, and Dilma's first term, this rose to 16–17% but has now dropped back to less than 14%, by any standards a very low power base from which to lead a stable coalition (see Table 4). It had no choice but to form a coalition. There was – and still is – fierce rivalry between the PT and the PSDB, the third largest party in the Chamber, with 54 deputies.

The PSDB, *Partido da Social Democracia do Brasil*, Brazil's Social Democratic Party, is a formerly left-leaning party

Table 4 PT Federal deputies 1999–2019

Legislative term	Number of PT deputies	Percentage of total deputies
1999–2003	59	11.5
2003–2007	91	17.3
2007–2011	83	16.1
2011–2015	88	17.1
2015–2019	69	13.4

Source: http://pt.wikipedia.org/wiki/Partido_dos_Trabalhadores.

which swung to the right in the 1990s and, during the presidency of the former Marxist sociologist, Fernando Henrique Cardoso, implemented an IMF-backed programme of sweeping privatisations and government cuts.

An alliance with the PSDB was almost unthinkable, so the PT had little option but seek to form a coalition with the PMDB *Partido do Movimento Democrático Brasileiro* or Brazilian Democratic Movement Party, Brazil's largest party, which has 66 deputies, only three fewer than the PT.

The PMDB or 'physiological' party

The PMDB keeps a strangely low profile: it has not fielded a presidential candidate for 12 years and has no real policies (apart from being broadly in favour of the status quo). It is the party best summed up by a strange yet apt Brazilian word *fisiológico* (physiological), well defined in 2007 by a US diplomat in an internal State Department cable, made available through Wikileaks: 'a pejorative term denoting a person or party for sale, always seeking personal advantage' (Hunt, 2015). The PMDB is a continuation of the MDB *Movimento Democrático Brasileiro* or Brazilian Democratic Movement, a party created by the generals during the dictatorship to provide a façade of democracy. The MDB, at the time the only permitted opposition party, was far more successful in the elections than the military had expected and was prepared to tolerate, so in their final decade in power the generals altered the electoral rules to create a solid bloc of support for the pro-government party, Arena (*Aliança Renovadora Nacional,* National Renovation Alliance). Ironically, after the dictatorship ended, this was the electoral space that PMDB occupied and still occupies, which means that their representation in Congress is always far greater than their electoral strength warrants.

Since the return to democracy in 1985, the PMDB has participated in every government except the disastrous Collor de Mello administration (1990–1992), the demise of which may have been partly provoked by the President's audacity in excluding it. With its slogan, 'the Party of Brazil', it projects an image of benign stability but is seen by many as a distasteful relic of the dictatorship. It is a clever political operator, demanding ministries, jobs and concessions for powerful Congressional groups (such as the *ruralistas*, the conservative landowning bloc) in return for its support of the government of the day. It has been a real headache for the PT and has long blocked any attempt to carry out much-needed political reform.

Mass mobilization sidelined

The only way to survive without PMDB support in 2002 would have been for the PT to use its considerable mobilizing capacity to organize mass demonstrations in favour of radical political reform. But this would have been a very risky tactic, especially at a time when foreign investors and bankers were very wary of the PT and might have provoked a crisis similar to the one then confronting neighbouring Argentina, which was suffering a severe recession after massive capital flight and a debt default. Moreover, some analysts, like university lecturer Pablo Ortellado, believe that by 2002 the PT was too far down the electoral road to change course. According to him, 'The party made a definitive option to choose the institutional route to power, to stand in elections for mayor, governor, president, to conquer political power. This option had a strong demobilizing impact, particularly at the end of the 1980s. And throughout the 1990s we saw a sharp decline in mobilization, which had been running at a very high level (Ortellado, 2014).'

Indeed, there is nothing to suggest that Lula seriously thought of bringing the masses on to the streets, though some PT politicians were proposing it. For him, the safer route of negotiation meant that he could deploy his considerable bargaining skills, developed while he was a trade union leader. This meant, in practice, that the party had to play by the old rules of the game – and that meant buying votes. Further down the road this tactic, so alien to the PT's genesis, would cost them dearly and implicate them in a series of scandals.

The PT tackles poverty

Once in power, Lula and his advisers began rapidly to move the country away from the extreme neo-liberal policies of the Fernando Henrique Cardoso administration, and to rebuild the state, significantly diminished under the previous government, so that it would re-assert its position at the heart of national decision-making and intervene to resolve the country's social problems (Zibechi, 2014: ch.3). In time, the manner in which this policy was implemented profoundly altered the PT's relationship with social movements, although that was not the intention.

The government defined widespread extreme poverty as the country's most pressing social problem. One of Lula's first measures was to merge several social welfare initiatives into a single programme, called *Bolsa Família*, under which the poorest families receive monthly cash payments, provided they enrol their children at school. By 2012, the programme had 15 million beneficiaries – about one in every four families (Soares, 2012). Alongside this programme, the PT government also increased the real value of the minimum wage, the benchmark for the wages paid to poorer workers. It went up by almost 50% in a decade, compared with a 25% rise for the average wage over the same period (Loman et al., 2014). Employers were encouraged to register their workers, a legal requirement that until then had been widely flouted. The boom in construction for public infrastructure projects and for private residential blocks, stimulated by the increased availability of mortgages made possible by low inflation, absorbed hundreds of thousands of unskilled workers. With almost full employment in some regions and with a sympathetic government, workers felt more confident in demanding that their rights be respected, including the obligation on the employer to register them.

Inequality of income

The jobs boom allowed many to find a way out of extreme poverty through regular, paid labour. Although these families have made huge strides over the last decade, they are still far from affluent. Indeed, the sociologist Jessé Souza thinks it is misleading to describe them as 'middle class' because they are so different from the established middle class. They have shown extraordinary grit and single-minded dedication, says Souza, struggling against the odds in a labour market characterized by permanent insecurity and intense competition. Even though they have faced considerable prejudice from the wealthier sectors of society, many have succeeded in getting themselves 'included in capitalism', that is, they have become consumers of goods such as televisions, refrigerators and mobile phones.

They have been helped by the networks of support they have created through their extended families and the churches, particularly the rapidly-expanding evangelical churches. Souza says they are today a step above the 'unproductive' and 'doomed' *ralé* (rabble or lumpen proletariat), which, he says, still account for almost a third of the population, but their standard of living still falls well short of that of the established, largely white middle classes, who emerged during the second half of the 20th century (Souza, 2009: 15–71). He has coined a term for the 30 million new consumers – the *classe batalhadora* (the struggling class) (Machado, 2011).

The Fundação Getúlio Vargas, a highly respected academic institution, has had a go at calculating the scale of the change in the country's social structure, basing some of its figures on projections, rather than hard data, which is as yet unavailable. It believes that today most – 147.1 million people – of the country's population belong to a broad group composed of the A, B or C classes, that is, people with a monthly income of more than two minimum wages, that is, R$1,448 (US$446, £381) (Neri, 2012). This means that the number of people in this group has nearly doubled from its level of 79.1 million in 2003. To a large extent, this impressive expansion is not due to population expansion or immigration, but comes from lifting people out of poverty; during the same period, the number of people in the group encompassing the D and E classes (that is, with a monthly income of under two minimum wages) fell to 48.9 million, just over half of its combined size in 2003 (ibid.). This remarkable reshaping of the country, achieved in little more than a decade, reduced the level of social inequality in Brazil, with the Gini index falling from 0.553 in 2002 to 0.500 in 2011 (Studart, 2013). Brazil bucked the global trend towards increasing social inequality and this won plaudits for the PT and contributed to Lula's re-election in 2006.

However, social inequality, still running at one of the highest rates in the world, has been lessened, not resolved. Brazil still ranks as the 16th most unequal country in the world (CIA, 2014). Over 16 million people have a per capita income of one *real (R$1)* a day (Pomar, W, 2014) – in April 2015 1 *real* was worth about 22p or US$0.34. Another 30 million earn at most 2–3 *reais* a day (ibid.). As the minimum salary today stands at R$788, or R$26 a day, this means that more than a fifth of the population still lives in poverty or extreme poverty. At the other end of the spectrum, 5,000 individuals each have assets of over R$60 m (US$18.7 m, £12.5 m). They have a total wealth of R$1.7 tn (US$520 bn, £350 bn), which is more than a third of Brazil's 2013 GNP of R$4.8 tn (US$1.5 tn, £1.0 tn) (ibid.).

It has been pointed out, that even if inequality were to carry on declining at the same pace as it has over the last decade, it would still take a further 20 years to bring it down to the level current in the USA, itself one of the most unequal countries of the OECD (Loman, 2014).

Social injustice

Moreover, it is questionable whether the poorer classes in Brazil are treated with greater social justice, despite the welcome improvement in their income level. A completely just nation would be one in which the human rights of all people – irrespective of race, gender or income – would be respected equally and they would all have the same access to education, public health and security. This utopia does not exist anywhere but some countries, like the Scandinavian nations and Cuba, come close. Slavery existed longer in Brazil than anywhere else in the Americas and its legacy of racism, gross inequality and lack of social justice is hard to eradicate. The police continue to treat poor people in marginal areas very differently from the rich, with a policy of 'shoot first, ask afterwards'. According to the United Nations, between 2003 and 2009 the police in Rio de Janeiro and São Paulo were implicated in at least 11,000 so-called 'resistance killings' – in which the victims were shot after allegedly opening fire on police. Evidence shows that many of these deaths were unlawful killings (Amnesty International, 2013). 'Our police still have blood on their hands, and are allowed to act with impunity as extra-judicial killings remain rife in Brazil's major cities,' said Atila Roque, director of Amnesty International's Brazil office (ibid.). Discrimination against indigenous communities and gay people is also widespread.

Access to education and healthcare

Experts agree that the long-term solution to the violence and to discrimination is improved access to education, greater social mobility and affirmative action. The PT administrations have achieved significant advances. Brazilian children are staying longer at school, though the quality of the teaching often leaves much to be desired. It is easier for poor students to go to university; in 2005, the then Minister of Education, Tarso Genro, created Pro-Uni (*Programa Universidade para Todos*, University for All Programme), which by 2013 had provided 1.2 million university scholarships for poor students. Quotas have been established for black and poor students at some universities, though this has been controversial. So progress is being made, though more slowly than many Brazilians would like.

Dissatisfaction is more widespread with the public health services, which are administered by often inefficient municipal and state governments (Costa, 2014). The health service in rural areas has long suffered from a severe shortage of doctors. This is largely because the profession has traditionally been monopolized by the established middle classes, who are the only Brazilians with the resources to fund the long training. Few of the qualified doctors have then been willing to work in Brazil's poorer hinterland, either remote rural areas or big city slums. To combat the problem, the government set up in 2012 a programme called Mais Médicos (More Doctors), to attract doctors to work in these underprivileged areas by offering decent salaries. Although the programme was open to Brazilians, the majority of the doctors (5,400 out of 6,500) came from Cuba, under the auspices of the Pan American Health Organization (Caulyt, 2014). The programme was attacked by Brazilian medical associations, who wanted to maintain the closed shop system, even when it means depriving millions of access to health care. Attempts were made to undermine it, by highlighting the cases of half a dozen Cuban doctors who complained about their salaries. They receive only R$3,000 (US$919, £623) of the R$10,000 (US$2,077) paid to the Cuban government, plus free accommodation – and these few wanted to leave the programme. However the overwhelming majority have continued in their posts, bringing medical care to people who had none before.

So change is coming but, once again, more slowly than many Brazilians would like. It was interesting to see that in the protests that unexpectedly erupted in mid-2013 people were not calling for higher wages but for improved public services and for better treatment from the authorities. The posters demanded 'FIFA standards of health and education' (a reference to the luxury football stadiums that were being built for the World Cup) and to be treated 'with respect'.

The changing face of trade unionism

Remarkable as it may seem, after a decade of PT government, there are fewer effective channels than in the past through which poor Brazilians can fight for their rights, including their right to greater social justice. This is because through the CUT (*Central Única dos Trabalhadores*, Unified Workers' Central) many of the trade unions, which led the struggle for democracy and for better working conditions in the 1980s and 1990s, have thrown in their lot with the government and largely relinquished their role of protecting the rights of the poorest workers, though they still defend the interests of the labour élite which comprises workers in established industries in the richer areas of the country. It is not so much that they have been co-opted but that they have become part of the ruling power group.

Their incorporation into the government did not happen by accident. When he became president, Lula felt that senior trade unionists, with whom he had worked for decades, were one of the few groups he could trust and he wanted to place them in key positions. During his first term, approximately half of all senior positions in government – around 1,305 vacancies – were held by trade unionists, and together they controlled an annual budget of R$200 bn [US$61.5 bn, £42 bn] (Fakier and Ehmke, 2014). At the same time, trade-union-backed deputies emerged as an effective bloc in Congress. They repeatedly acted as a counterweight to the right during the first Dilma government, even though, with just 91 seats compared with 273 in the hands of the pro-business bloc, there were limits to what they could achieve.

Pension funds

However, the PT-trade union alliance went far further than this. As the Uruguayan writer and activist Raúl Zibechi argues in a recent book on Brazil, together they had decided, before they came to power, that they would 'moralize' capitalism by making it work more effectively for the poor. One of their tactics was to find a way of generating large flows of capital which they could use for this purpose without restrictions (Zibechi, 2014). Shortly after he came to power, Lula attended a conference convened by the leading three pension funds (Previ, Petros and Funcef) and called on the trade unions to work with these groups to set up specific pension funds for workers. This policy would have two main benefits: unionized workers would get good pensions on retirement; and the government would obtain money for investment (ibid.). The policy has been extraordinarily successful; the number of groups (trade unions, cooperatives and professional associations) setting up pensions funds increased from seven in 2003 to 476 in 2010. By that year pension fund assets were worth 16% of GDP and trade union representatives were installed on the board of the country's largest pension funds (ibid.).

The Development Bank (BNDES)

The government also ensured that trade unionists, as trusted allies, would play an important role in the administration of the country's large state-owned bank, the BNDES (*Banco Nacional de Desenvolvimento Econômico e Social*, National Bank of Social and Economic Development). They planned to expand its role as one of the main channels for the state to intervene in the economy. It was appropriate for the unionists to get involved, because FAT (*Fundo de Amparo ao Trabalhador*, Worker Assistance Fund), a worker unemployment fund administered by the Ministry of Labour which derives its income from a tax on company revenue and a duty on imports, supplies 40% of BNDES capital. The bank's assets grew fourfold from 2007, reaching R\$814 billion (US\$286bn, £179bn) in 2014 (Leahy, 2015). Its disbursements that year were R\$190 billion (US\$67bn, £42bn), more than the total annual output of neighbouring Uruguay. Today it is the largest development bank in the world (BNDES, no date), and one of the most unaccountable financial institutions on the planet. A special network, Plataforma BNDES, has been set up by Brazilian non-governmental organizations to try and monitor its activities.

With these additional resources, BNDES was entrusted with the mission of creating 'Brazilian champions' – private companies, similar to South Korean *chaebols* – which would be able to take on the world's largest multinationals. Paying little attention to small or medium-sized companies, the BNDES singled out economic groups, already big, that it believed could expand rapidly and compete successfully at home and abroad. It provided heavily subsidized loans – with interest rates at about half the level available from traditional credit sources – to large engineering companies (such as Odebrecht, OAS, Camargo Corrêa and Andrade Gutierrez) and to agribusiness (such as the ethanol giant, Cosan).

The bank also bought shares in key companies. BNDES and its share-holding arm, BNDESPar, hold about 17% of Petrobrás, while BNDESPar alone owns 8% of Vale, the world's biggest iron ore exporter, and 24% of JBS, the world's largest meatpacker (Leahy, 2015).

This policy has been successful in creating giant Brazilian companies (and strengthening Brazilian subsidiaries of foreign companies), which have increased exports and won large contracts abroad, particularly in the field of construction, but it has also been controversial, even within the business sector. It is seen as channelling taxpayers' money to the rich and powerful, exacerbating inequalities, distorting the economy and encouraging cronyism.

Indeed, the BNDES is expensive to run: its subsidies cost the government more than Bolsa Família, earning the bank the nickname Bolsa Empresário, or 'tycoon grant'. The BNDES also has funded spectacular failures. The most remarkable was the case of businessman Eike Batista, the son of a minister of mines and energy under the Goulart and Collor administrations, whose oil, mining and logistics companies received generous subsidies from BNDES. Batista was Brazil's richest man – and even boasted once that he would shortly overtake Carlos Slim of Mexico to become the richest man in the world – until his empire imploded spectacularly in 2013. His US$35 billion (£23bn) fortune crumbled and today, with his outstanding debts of US$2 billion (£1.3bn), he has joined the select club of 'negative billionaires' (Yang, 2015). Moreover, many of the companies that have benefited from BNDES largesse are today embroiled in the current Petrobrás scandal, which may well become the largest corruption scandal in Brazil's history.

Foreign policy

Along with promoting Brazil's economic presence abroad, Lula also radically changed Brazil's foreign policy. Key here was his opposition to the Free Trade Area of the Americas (FTAA), President George Bush (Senior)'s plan for turning the whole of the Americas into a single free trade area under US control, a proposal which had had the support of Lula's predecessor, President Fernando Henrique Cardoso. Instead, in alliance with Venezuela and, to some extent, Argentina – the PT government promoted the idea that South America is an autonomous geopolitical region, separate from the United States and not subordinate to US hegemony (Fox, 2010). It took measures to strengthen Mercosur, the trade alliance with Brazil's neighbours, and supported the formation of Unasur (Union of South American Nations), a regional political body which does not include the USA.

Not surprisingly, the US government did not welcome these changes, particularly the incorporation of Venezuela into Mercosur (Fitzpatrick, 2011). It repeatedly refused to back Brazil's attempt to gain a permanent seat on the UN Security Council, something that rankled the Lula government (Arraes, 2015).

Not one to be intimidated, Lula responded with spirit, saying on one occasion that he was developing alliances with countries like India, China and Russia to 'block the imperialist's geographical advance' (Brant, 2004). For good measure, he added that the ties with these countries are 'visceral and based on common interests' because 'nobody wants the empire to survive' (ibid.).

Social movements

Lula's radical rhetoric abroad was, in part, a cover for his caution at home. Because of his reluctance to antagonize big economic groups and agribusiness, his government did not provide the anticipated support for popular and grass-roots movements, which grew weaker under his administration. While co-option may have played a role, with a few activists accepting positions in government ministries, Brazil's most powerful social movement, the MST (*Movimento dos Trabalhadores Rurais Sem Terra*, Landless Workers' Movement), largely retained its autonomy. Even so, its militancy declined, because many grass-root members, fervent supporters of Lula, accepted at face value the President's emotional appeal for their patience. On one occasion Lula came down the ramp of the Presidential Palace to speak to hundreds of MST activists who had marched on Brasília and were making militant demands for a radical programme of agrarian reform. Lula spoke to them directly: 'You have been waiting 500 years for a government that represents you. Please give me a few years to deliver the justice you need and deserve'. The slogan-shouting turned into applause, though not from the MST leaders. The government also made some attempt to create a form of 'participatory democracy' in which the views of social movements were canvassed but the scheme faltered, after activists discovered that almost invariably, when there were conflicting demands, the government sided with the powerful economic and agribusiness lobbies.

This intermeshing of the interests of the government and the labour movement had important political consequences. Now the trade union movement was effectively part of the government, it became fearful of supporting actions and campaigns by social movements if these could threaten the survival of the government. It failed to mobilize its members even when the Lula government passed a controversial pension reform that reduced worker benefits and it became more reluctant to support strike action in general, fearful of disrupting its cosy relationship with big business.

Labour disputes

But, of course, Brazil still needs a militant, mobilized trade union movement. Millions of workers still labour under poor conditions in many sectors, including the meat-packing, cattle and poultry industries. This sector employs some 800,000 workers, over a fifth of whom suffer from work-related health problems (IHU Online, 2011). 'Today a young man aged 25 to 30 with five or six years' work experience is showing signs of acute pain and permanent impairment', said a trade unionist (ibid.). There are also thousands of unskilled workers employed on building sites for the large hydroelectric dams being constructed in the Amazon and on other big infrastructure projects financed by the government's investment programmes – PAC 1 (*Programa de Aceleração do Crescimento 1*, Growth Acceleration Programme 1), announced in January 2007 with a budget of R$291 m (US$94 m, £64 m); and PAC 2 with the even heavier investment of R$959 m (US$310 m, £250 m), representing annual investment of about 5% of GNP each year.

There have been serious labour conflicts on the sites of the dams but the workers have seldom received adequate support from the trade unions. One emblematic case was a strike in 2011 on the site of the huge Belo Monte dam, being built on the Xingu River in the state of Pará in the Amazon. Ruy Sposato, from the *Movimento Xingu Vivo para Sempre* (Xingu Alive for Ever Movement), who spent seven months in the region, reported that a strike had erupted in early November, when four workers had refused to move heavy timber, claiming that the work was dangerous and their contract did not oblige them to carry out this kind of labour. After some turmoil, with workers threatening to set fire to buildings, the company backed down. A few days later, however, it abruptly sacked 138 workers and arranged for 40 policemen from Altamira to be despatched to the site where they forced all but one of the dismissed workers to board a bus which took them back to their state of origin, Maranhão.

This heavy-handed action provoked further unrest, with workers demanding a range of improvements. These included better catering arrangements on site, as over 200 workers had suffered from food poisoning because the food often arrived half-rotten, after being transported in unrefrigerated lorries along unpaved roads from Altamira, 50 kilometres away. Officially, the workers were represented in the dispute by the Pará branch of the *Sindicato de Trabalhadores da Construção Pesada* (Union of Heavy Construction Workers) but the workers did not trust the union, as they had no representative of their own on the union board.

Perhaps their suspicions were well-founded, for when a union representative eventually arrived he came with a representative of the federal government, who had flown up from Brasília, and together they put pressure on the workers to suspend the strike, even though the company had only promised 'talks'. Reluctantly the workers agreed, though warning that a further strike could erupt 'at any moment'. Sposato commented: 'From now there will be two sides: the workers who want improvements; and the traditional union, the government and the company, who form an alliance pressing for an end to strikes (Fachin, 2011).'

Despite the ongoing worker grievances, the official labour movement's close relations with the PT government combined with the generous wage increases that Lula was authorizing for public sector employees, led to a dramatic fall in the number of strikes. In 1989, a high point in a decade of massive labour struggle, there were nearly 4,000 strikes in a single year; that was more than the combined total for the eight years of the two Lula administrations (Zibechi, 2014: 257). However, the number rose again under Dilma. Nearly 80,000 workers went on strike on PAC sites alone in 2011 (Zibechi, 2014: 254). In the second half of 2012, with the economy weakening, which made it harder for the government to authorise large wage increases, there was a surge in strike activity in the public sector, which the government dealt with firmly (BBC, 2012 and Reuters, 2012).

The PT's Faustian pact

From the start it was clear that the PT would pay a high political price for remaining in government. For many PT veterans, who had spent the best years of their life in the long struggle to get Lula elected president, it was a bitter blow to see their Workers' Party cosying up to the same right-wing politicians who had supported the military government and done everything in the early years to destroy the party. Men like Senator José Sarney, a landowner and head of an oligarchy in Maranhão state, who became President unexpectedly in 1985, after the much more widely respected President-elect, Tancredo Neves, died suddenly, just before his inauguration; and Paulo Maluf, ex-governor and ex-mayor of São Paulo, wanted by Interpol for stealing public funds, but still, amazingly elected and re-elected to Congress.

Even so, many staunch *petistas* were visibly shaken when the *mensalão* scandal erupted in June 2005. In an explosive interview with the *Folha de S. Paulo* newspaper, federal deputy Roberto Jefferson revealed that the PT had been paying a number of deputies R\$30,000 (US\$12,000, £9,000) every month to get them to vote for government bills. He said the money came from the advertising budgets of state-owned companies, all of them headed by PT appointees, and that those who received the bribe called it the *mensalão*, meaning a large monthly payment. The term quickly became the popular label for the scandal.

Over the following weeks there was a flurry of press reports of further scandals, including the claim that private companies were paying bribes to win contracts in the state sector. In July the brother of the Workers' Party

President, José Genoíno, was seized at an airport with some R$100,000 (US$40,000, £30,000) in his pants and more money in his suitcase. The press had a field day and the scandal topped the news bulletins day after day. The government was forced to hold a parliamentary enquiry and, after many more twists and turns, the scandal finished up in the Supreme Court. In October 2012, after a long televised trial, José Dirceu, José Genoino and the PT treasurer, Delúbio Soares, were found guilty of the crime of bribery (*corrupção passiva*) and sent to prison.

Brazilians have long known that politics is a dirty game and that politicians use their position to acquire large fortunes. Back in the 1950s the politician Adhemar de Barros, who was twice elected governor of São Paulo state, became renowned for a slogan coined by one of his supporters: *'Adhemar rouba mas faz'* (Adhemar steals but he gets things done) – a catchphrase that makes most Brazilians smile wryly.

Given this, it might seem surprising that the *mensalão* caused such a furore. There is no doubt that the rumpus was partly manufactured by the right-wing parties, which were delighted at catching the PT with its trousers down (literally in the airport incident), because the party had boasted for so many years that it was 'different', that it was 'ethical', that it was changing the political culture and setting new standards. But the scandal cannot be brushed off as right-wing propaganda. Even though they knew that the party had made compromises, many *petistas* had thought that it was still striving to develop a new political culture and had set ethical standards. As a result, they felt deeply betrayed.

The scandal hurt the PT badly, with some politicians forced to resign and others failing to win re-election, but Lula himself emerged relatively unscathed. There was never any concrete proof of his involvement (although many Brazilians find it hard to believe that he did not know what was going on). More important was the fact that many poor Brazilians, particularly in the northeast, regard the federal capital of Brasília as a far-off, incomprehensible place, which they don't trust. What is crucial for them – and much more real than a media scandal – is the improvement in their lives under the PT administrations, and that alone is enough to ensure their loyalty.

Development at all costs

Another area where the PT governments, both under Lula and Dilma, have disappointed many of their supporters has been their blind devotion to 'development' at all costs. Perhaps because the party was founded by trade unionists, who grew up in the 1950s and 1960s when the dream of every migrant arriving in São Paulo was to work for the Volkswagen car factory, it has an old-fashioned, simplistic view of 'progress', which makes it unsympathetic to the indigenous and environmental causes.

It has accepted the right-wing mantra that the indigenous peoples (who number a few hundred thousand) have too much land and that land would be more productive in the hands of agribusiness, which would use it to boost the country's exports. The idea that biodiversity and standing forest could be far more profitable than soya – something that studies have shown time and again – has yet to reach the higher echelons of the party, and it still refuses to listen to scientists who are increasingly warning that the scale of the environmental damage in Brazil, particularly in the Amazon basin, is harming Brazil's climate and compromising the country's long-term future.

PT governments have stubbornly pushed ahead with huge projects of infrastructure development, despite growing signs that these projects are environmentally unsustainable and are damaging the lives of thousands of poor Brazilians, the very people whom the party is supposed to represent. It is noticeable that, while in the northeast the PT retains great support among poor sectors of the population, it is widely disliked among the rural populations of the Amazon, who associate it with big development projects that ride roughshod over their lives. Activists in the Amazon have often told us that Dilma's administration has been the 'worst government' since the return to civilian rule in 1985.

An emblematic case concerns the 13,000 Munduruku Indians who live beside the Tapajós river in the Amazon, where the government is deliberately sabotaging their efforts to gain land rights, because the area they are claiming is due to be flooded when the first of the seven hydro-electric dams planned for the Tapajós river is built. If the Munduruku were to have their rights to this land recognized – as Funai, the government's indigenous agency, admits they should – it would be almost impossible to evict them because indigenous land rights are inviolable, according to the country's progressive Constitution, approved in 1988 during the heady years following the return to democratic rule after 25 years of dictatorship.

Land and tax reform shelved

The PT's pragmatic decision to work with parties across the political spectrum has meant concentrating on a few policies, mainly geared to alleviating poverty and improving social welfare, and giving up on many of its earlier, more radical ideas for structural change. In his first year in power, Lula firmly rejected the proposal, made by an MST ally, Plínio de Arruda Sampaio, for the government to carry out a wide-ranging, radical programme of agrarian reform (Carter, 2015).

The PT has made no serious attempt to reduce income inequality by introducing progressive taxation. As well as abandoning earlier proposals to tax large fortunes, it failed to correct the present income tax, which takes a disproportionate amount from low- and middle-income workers, with no higher rate for those on much larger incomes. In addition, no effort has been made to change Brazil's ICMS (*Imposto sobre Circulação de Mercadorias e Prestação de Serviços*, Tax on the Circulation of Goods and Services), a value-added tax levied by state governments, which obtains much of its revenue from taxing basic foodstuffs. This means that the poorest section of the population, who spend a higher proportion of their income on food, pay more tax.

Instead of attacking tax inequality, at least by making the tax system more transparent, the PT has concentrated instead on poverty relief and raising the incomes of the low paid. This has had the paradoxical effect of bringing many more people above the threshold to pay income-tax, and into the bracket which is taxed at an unfairly high rate.

Left-of-centre parties elected with high expectations almost invariably disappoint – one only has to think of Tony Blair's victory in the UK in 1997 and François Hollande's electoral triumph in France in 2012. Perhaps more was expected from Lula because of his extraordinary personal story and his role in forcing the military out of power. But the combination of a demobilized labour movement, corruption, weak environmental policies, and a failure to undertake structural reform, including political reform, meant that many erstwhile *petistas* were happy to join in the wave of protests that swept across the country in 2013.

The 2013 protests

The first signs of widespread political discontent came in June 2013, when Brazil was suddenly rocked by a series of massive protests. Hundreds of thousands filled the streets, demanding better transport, health, education, and housing. Their homemade placards demanded an end to corruption and proclaimed their disenchantment with government and politicians, at all levels and of all hues. They carried banners saying 'No political party represents me', a sign of the alienation provoked by the corrupt practices and spurious alliances of the political parties, including now the PT, which has led to the generalized feeling that 'politicians are all the same'.

In Brasília they marched on Congress and the ministries; in São Paulo they demonstrated in front of the governor's palace; and in Rio de Janeiro they camped in front of the city council. The protests seemed to come out of nowhere and took everyone – government, opposition, political parties, unions, media and pundits – completely by surprise, because they had bypassed traditional intermediaries. They were, in fact, the first mass event in Brazil to be organized almost entirely on social media.

The catalyst was the protest against a proposed rise in bus fares called by the small, student-based MPL – *Movimento Passe Livre* (Free Fare Movement), previously unknown to the general public, against the background of the costly, over-budget preparations for the 2014 World Cup extravaganza, including new state-of-the-art stadiums, one even located in the rainforest capital of Manaus, which has no football tradition. There was a panicked response from the politicians at this unexpected show of 'people power', conjuring up as it did visions of mob rule. In Brasília members of Congress from all parties queued up at the microphones to declare fervently that they were listening to the 'clamour of the streets', and to show their zeal they worked late into the night, voting on bills which had languished on the shelf for months or even years. Dilma called emergency meetings to address the issues raised by the protesters and invited the young students of the MPL to the presidential palace to listen to what they had to say – an unprecedented step for someone who rarely listens even to her own ministers. Municipal authorities up and down the country cancelled fare increases.

A group of anarchists calling themselves Black Blocs infiltrated some of the protests and attacked banks and public buildings, smashing windows and breaking cash machines, the symbols of capitalism. Although they were a small minority, clearly identified by their black clothing, masks and balaclavas, the police used the threat of the Black Blocs to justify the use of aggressive tactics, such as kettling, and indiscriminate arrests. The protests eventually abated, in part because many people became afraid of being caught up in violence.

Origins of the protest movements

An indication of the distance that had arisen between the PT government and the social movements can be gauged by a closer look at the organizations behind the protests. The MPL had been founded by political activists, many of whom had cut their political teeth in the anti-globalization movement. At first, MPL was almost exclusively supported by students, for whom the price of the bus fare was important, as many spent a third of their income or more on public transport. For ten years it had been organizing protests around fare increases in cities all over the country – Salvador, Florianópolis, Goiânia, Vitória and elsewhere (Ortellado, 2014). A protest in Florianópolis in 2004 mobilized 15,000–20,000 people, about 4% of the total population of 400,000 – an impressive achievement, though it was largely ignored by the national press (Pomar, 2013). In time, the MPL evolved, moving beyond student issues to campaign against all the main forms of discrimination – around class, gender, race and age (Zibechi, 2014: 274–81). One key decision was to work more in poorer areas, which led to a broadening of their base.

Another key organization, which had begun working in poor neighbourhoods before the MPL, was the Comitê Popular da Copa (Popular Committee for the World Cup), which emerged in the run up to the 2007 Pan American Games in Rio de Janeiro, campaigning against the forced relocation of families. It organized 47 demonstrations between April 2006 and October 2007. For the Comitê, the way the Games were organized proved that the government was not prepared to manage public funds in a democratic and transparent fashion. It was an indication, it believed, of what would happen when the far bigger investments for the World Cup and the Olympics were made – a prediction that is being largely borne out by events (Zibechi, 2014: 281).

Like the MPL, the Comitê carried out meticulous research and in June 2012 it provided the data for a report published by a coalition of local committees, which denounced the infringement of the right to housing of 170,000 people and strongly criticized 'the systematic disregard for the law and for environmental rights, workers' rights, the right to work, and consumers' rights' (National Coalition, 2012). The report also made a complaint with a familiar ring to many people in other parts of the world: it attacked the public-private partnerships being set up to carry out much of the construction work, saying: 'The public gets stuck with the costs, while private firms reap the profits. (ibid.)'

Both the MPL and the Comitê are the product of a new political culture, one that is very different from the bureaucratic and somewhat hierarchical culture of the traditional labour movement. While the PT and the main trade union body, the CUT, were formed during the struggle against the military dictatorship in the 1970s and were marked by the need for discipline, loyalty and secrecy, the MPL and the Comitê arose at a time when many young people and activists in poor areas felt alienated from the trade unions and the PT. The guiding principles of these new organizations are very different – collective leadership and consensus. Not surprisingly, relations with the PT have been strained; in 2002 a PT-linked youth group called JR (*Juventude Revolução*, Youth Revolution) expelled a faction that was demanding that the group take its own decisions outside the control of the PT leadership (Pomar, 2013). This breakaway faction helped to organize the highly successful protest in Florianópolis in 2004 and eventually became part of MPL.

The MPL and the Comitê were far from being the only groups involved in the mushrooming of protests in June 2013, when it is estimated that some 5% of the population of Brazil – one in every 20 – took to the streets at one time or another, but they were the most important.

Media response

At first, mass media coverage of the protests was extremely hostile. The university lecturer, Pablo Ortellado, monitored the reporting: 'We looked systematically at the main newspapers (*Folha de S. Paulo*, *Estado de S. Paulo* and *Globo*), the four main weekly magazines and the TV coverage. It was all very critical. The mobilization was attacked on all sides. (Ortellado, 2014)' Early on 13 June, all the mass media called for stronger intervention from the police. 'It was clearly organized', comments Ortellado. 'Time and again the TV presenter looked at the camera and called for the police to intervene to contain the *baderneiros* (troublemakers) of the MPL.' It seemed as if the media were paving the way for a much tougher clampdown on the protests by the authorities.

But suddenly the tone of the coverage changed, becoming much more sympathetic to the demonstrators. It has become accepted wisdom that this change occurred after scenes of police brutality were shown on television, which aroused widespread sympathy for the protesters. However, this turns out to be a simplification. The about-turn happened a few hours *before* the images of violence were broadcast. The catalyst was an opinion poll, carried out by *Folha de S. Paulo* newspaper, which showed that three-quarters of the population supported the demonstrators. The way the media responded to the poll's findings is an interesting example of how, even in a country like Brazil, where most newspapers and TV stations are conservative and openly anti-PT, they will not back views seen by the public to be extreme and unfair.

The protests subsided and some people now see them as a failure. But Ortellado disagrees: 'Research from the *Folha de S. Paulo* shows that in 70% of cities with over 200,000 inhabitants the authorities reduced fares. That is an extraordinary victory. And in numerous small towns in the interior, which have 10,000 or 20,000 inhabitants, the population occupied the town halls to demand a fare reduction. And they often succeeded. All this changes people. When someone living in São Paulo who took part in the demonstrations gets on a bus and sees that the fare has fallen once again to three *reais*, he thinks: "I achieved that". It has a psychological impact, greatly strengthening social struggle.'

Police repression

The protests produced results but, as has already been noted, they also provoked a violent response from the police, particularly the PM (*Polícia Militar*, Military Police), which acquired a reputation for brutality during the military dictatorship and has never been reformed. Between 2009 and 2014, a total of just over 11,000 people were killed by the police in Brazil, mainly by the PM, an average of five a day, according to the NGO Brazilian Forum on Public Security (*Forum Brasileiro de Segurança Publica*) (Amnesty International, 2013). Faced with an unprecedented level of mobilization on the streets, the police responded with more violence. Eliane Brum, one of Brazil's leading independent journalists, says that successive PT governments have done little to curb this:

> Douglas Rodrigues, 17 years old, a third year college student who worked in a snack bar, was a victim of political violence. He received a shot in his chest from a policeman in the afternoon of 27 October [2013], when he was standing at a bar with his 13-year-old brother in Vila Medeiros in São Paulo. He only had time to say a single sentence, which has become a symbol against the genocide of generations of poor, black youngsters in the poor outskirts of Brazil's cities. This was Douglas's last sentence, a set of vowels and consonants containing a whole life, uttered before he fell down dead: 'Why did you shoot me?' In protest over his death, the local inhabitants set

light to buses, cars and lorries, and damaged some bank agencies.

He – and many like him – have become the new 'disappeared'. They are paying the price of democracy, now that Brazilians have taken democracy to the streets. This is why the two clenched fists of the two Josés – Genoíno and Dirceu [two veteran PT politicians, arrested for corruption in the *mensalão* scandal,] – are such a melancholy sight. It is a gesture that is outdated, incomplete. Lula, the PT and the top ranks of the government have spent time and energy in distancing themselves from these leaders. Perhaps they should spend more time listening to the new symbols forged in the protests (Brum, 2013).

Police repression was also much in evidence in 2014, as the authorities sought to prevent protesters taking advantage of the international attention being paid to Brazil as it staged the World Cup. For instance, on 2 July 2014, while the World Cup was in full swing, the MPL organized an open air meeting in the Praça de Sé, a square in the centre of São Paulo, to hold a public debate with Fernando Grella, Secretary for Public Security in the state government. Grella, predictably, did not turn up. Instead, before the meeting could even begin and with only about 150 people present, the square was surrounded by soldiers from the PM in full battle gear, equipped with tear gas and rubber bullets.

As one eye-witness reported, 'Without exaggeration, it seemed as if the PM was facing a foreign enemy, even though the 'enemy' was no more than ordinary citizens holding a debate and doing nothing else'. He went on to compare it to police actions at the height of the military dictatorship.

According to Pablo Ortellado, behaviour like this by the authorities had become routine. There had been an unwritten agreement between the media, the judiciary, the public ministry and all spheres of government, including the PT, he said, to repress all forms of protest during the World Cup: 'There has been an eerie silence about the suspension of those most basic of civil rights, the right to meet and the right to free expression. These rights have been simply suspended during the World Cup. Look in the *Globo*, the *Estado de S. Paulo, Época*. Nothing at all about what is going on' (Ortellado, 2014).

Other analysts agreed. Daniel Biral, a member of the group *Advogados Ativistas* (Activist Lawyers), said: 'What we have been seeing is radicalization, but not on the part of the social movements. We are seeing radicalization on the part of the state, which is repressing people in public squares instead of promoting public debate. The radicalization comes from the government' (Brito, 2014). Ortellado believes that the consequences for democracy will be severe: 'It is probably the most dangerous legacy of the World Cup.' He continues: 'If the PT thinks, because it has its roots in social movements, it can suspend such rights in view of the special circumstances, without leaving deep scars in society, it is very mistaken. We will live for a long time under the shadow of what has been going on' (ibid.).

While the PT could not be directly blamed for the behaviour of the military police forces which are run by the state governments – in this instance, by the PSDB-controlled government of São Paulo state – none of the activists believed that they had any effective way of making a formal complaint about the violation of their human rights. On the contrary, they maintained that the PT was condoning the violations. For while the central government funded some improvements to the police forces, they had no direct control over their tactics, and indeed, looked the other way when police violence took place.

The 2014 elections

Early on in the 2014 electoral campaign, the PT had expected to win easily, because approval rates for Dilma were high in many parts of the country. Moreover, right-wing groups did not have an obvious candidate with the charisma and the authority to challenge the PT's hold over a significant part of the electorate, particularly in the northeast, where Lula's welfare reforms had ensured a solid bedrock of support. One way for the opposition to challenge this was by choosing a candidate from that region. For a while, it seemed that tall and elegant Eduardo Campos might fit the bill. He was running for one of the smaller parties, the PSB (*Partido Socialista Brasileiro,* Brazilian Socialist Party) which, despite its name, is business-friendly. Campos was the grandson of a political legend, the left-wing populist Miguel Arraes, elected governor in 1962 with massive support from the cane-cutters he had helped to unionize. Forced into exile after the military coup in 1964, Arraes returned in triumph when the 1979 Amnesty Law relaxed the repression of the military dictatorship, and was twice more elected governor. But Arraes's popularity did not transfer to his urbane grandson, who lacked his maternal grandfather's popular touch and seemed to have more in common with his paternal grandfather – a right-wing sugar plantation owner, part of the rural oligarchy of Pernambuco.

The right switches candidates

With Campos's support hovering around 8–10 per cent, most of the right-wing groups decided, instead, to back Aécio Neves from the PSDB, another grandson of a famous man, Tancredo Neves. But the opinion polls suggested that Aécio was unlikely to defeat Dilma: he had proved an unpopular governor of the state of Minas Gerais with more than a whiff of corruption about him, as public money had been used to pay for an air strip which just happened to be close to his family's estate. It was a worrying time for the right, as it seemed that Dilma would cruise to victory.

The balance of forces changed dramatically in August 2014, after Eduardo Campos was killed when his small plane crashed in thick fog near Santos. With massive support from the dominant right-wing media, his running mate, Marina Silva, took over the candidacy and soared in the polls. She had resigned as environment minister from the Lula government in protest at the PT's failure to take environmental issues seriously, which gained her the support of many green voters. She was also an *evangélica*, a member of one of the powerful Pentecostal churches, which ensured her a large captive vote. For a while she came across as a saintly figure and, despite her time in government, as an outsider, who had not been tainted by the corruption and the *fisiologismo* of everyday political life in Brasília. She seemed to stand for the 'new politics' that thousands of protesters had called for in 2013 and she attracted many middle class voters who had been angered by the PT's involvement in corruption, which was reported in minute detail in the press (while equally shocking scandals involving the PSDB government in São Paulo state remained largely underreported).

The right promptly ditched Aécio Neves in favour of Marina Silva. For a while she could do no wrong. But, as the first round of the election approached, support for her wobbled and then fell as meteorically as it had at first soared. There were good reasons for this. It became clear to the general public that, with her lack of economic expertise, Marina was willing to work with hard-line free marketeers, who did not share the PT's commitment to income distribution. Marina's embrace of the socially conservative and, on occasions, homophobic attitudes of the evangelical churches also frightened some middle class voters. In the event, Aécio Neves comfortably won his place in the second round, with 34% of the vote against Marina's 21%.

The verdict of the foreign press

Dilma was ahead with 42 per cent but, as the second round approached, it became clear that the result would be tight. Much of the foreign press openly backed Aécio Neves: *The New York Times*, which invariably referred to Dilma Rousseff as 'a former guerrilla', reported just a few days before the election that 'investors have already voted with their *reais* and dollars – and it's Aécio Neves in a landslide' (Stewart, 2014); a few days earlier *The Economist* signalled its choice: 'Brazil needs growth and better government. Mr Neves is likelier to deliver these than Ms Rousseff is' (*The Economist*, 2014); and most crudely of all, *The Times* in London had run a story with the headline 'How to back Brazilian regime change' (Atherton, 2014).

This level of hostility towards Dilma from the right-wing foreign press might seem surprising, for the PT had stuck to orthodox economic policies and reserved a significant role for foreign investment. But the US establishment did not like the way the Lula government had wrecked its plans for the FTAA and conducted an independent foreign policy. In 2007 Lula said that the US simply could not accept Brazil becoming a world power. In 2008, he clearly expressed his displeasure at the US decision, after a gap of 58 years, to reactivate the US Fourth Fleet in Latin America and the Caribbean (Benson, 2008).

The partisan Brazilian press

Meanwhile, the domestic press, which almost entirely supported Aécio Neves, used murkier methods. In September a scandal erupted, with allegations that the huge state-owned oil company, Petrobrás, was routinely creaming 3% off its contracts and paying this money into a slush fund, which the government was using to buy votes in Congress. Allegations of this kind have been swirling around for years and they have involved all the main parties, but the right saw its chance to translate the widespread anger with corruption into an anti-Dilma vote.

Just a few days before the election, the country's most influential weekly magazine, the right-wing *Veja*, which has regularly been used in scurrilous anti-PT campaigns, rushed into print two days before its normal publication day, with an explosive cover story carefully timed to affect the outcome of the election. This carried a headline in large letters proclaiming *'Eles sabiam de tudo'* (They knew everything) – alongside pictures of Lula and Dilma. The story was based on an alleged confession from his prison cell by Alberto Youseff, known as the *doleiro* (currency dealer), who was collaborating with the prosecution in return for a lighter sentence. According to *Veja*, he accused both Lula and Dilma of knowing about the goings on in Petrobrás, something both had denied. No evidence was produced and even Youseff's own lawyer said he knew nothing about the confession.

Then on Sunday morning, just before the polls opened, a story circulated far and wide on social media that Yousseff had been poisoned, taken to hospital, and died. The implication was that an awkward witness had been bumped off to silence him. This story was denied by the Federal Police, which confirmed that he had, indeed, been hospitalized, but because of high blood pressure.

A close shave

These two stories almost certainly took votes from Dilma in São Paulo and the south, and may have contributed to the large number of abstentions. But they had little or no effect in the northeast where her vote remained solid. In the end Dilma squeaked home by a margin of 3.3 per cent, receiving 3.5 million votes more than Aécio, out of a total of 107 million, with 30 million abstentions. Ironically, if Aécio had managed to win a substantial majority of the 11.4 million votes in his home state of Minas Gerais, he might just have pulled it off: in fact, he lost in this state, obtaining 541,000 fewer votes than Dilma. Nationally, Dilma obtained 54.5 million votes, compared with Aécio's 51.0.

Everyone linked to the PT was shaken by the closeness of the result. Only at the eleventh hour did the social movements get out into the streets to campaign for Dilma, many of them very reluctantly. 'We voted for her because we realized that a victory for the opposition would be a huge setback', said Natália Szermeta, co-ordinator of the MTST (*Movimento dos Trabalhadores Sem-Teto*, Homeless Workers' Movement) (Senra, 2014).

An uncertain future

It was in this polarized atmosphere that Dilma took office, with serious difficulties on all fronts. The economy was faltering. Brazil's large current account deficit of US$86 billion, partly due to the fall in commodity prices on the world market, had deprived the government of the resources to repeat Lula's trick of increasing the minimum wage and making hefty investments in social welfare, while at the same time allowing bankers, construction companies and agribusiness to chalk up record profits.

Contradicting her pre-election assurance that she could sort out the country's economic problems without resorting to 'economic adjustment', Dilma selected the orthodox economist Joaquim Levy as her Finance Minister. To the dismay of many of her supporters, he applied classic austerity measures – reducing social spending, cutting subsidies, raising charges for public services, increasing interest rates, slashing labour rights and so on. Swingeing cuts were introduced in the budgets of the education, culture, science and other ministries. Large-scale job losses are expected. The impacts of this economic adjustment will be exacerbated by the negative effects of the present widespread drought on industry and agriculture.

Left-wing economists have long argued that Brazil could overcome its economic problems by adopting radically different policies, which would make the wealthy bear a far greater burden and reduce the social cost. However, there is no indication that Dilma is thinking of changing course. Her orthodox approach will not lead to economic recovery in the short term: according to ECLAC (Economic Commission for Latin America and the Caribbean), growth in Brazil was only 0.2 per cent in 2014 and it is not expected to be higher in 2015 or 2016.

A hostile Congress

At the same time, Congress lurched even further to the right as a result of the elections. Seven out of every ten elected federal deputies received campaign funding from at least one of the ten top funders, almost all from the engineering, mining, agribusiness and banking sectors. The weight of the law and order lobby has also grown. Early this year *The New York Times* ran a story in which it spoke of a 'major shift in Brazilian politics', with tough, right-wing politicians, generally linked to the police and the army, being elected across the country (Romero, 2015). The so-called *'bancada da bala'* (bullet caucus), emerged stronger, with 21 members in the national Congress alone.

There is no doubt Congress is skewed – over 70 per cent of its members are big farmers or businessmen, only 9 per cent are women, 8.5 per cent are black and fewer than 3 per cent are young (under 35 years old) (Betto, 2014). Although the right may have lost the presidential elections, it is more powerful and dangerous than ever before. Tarso Genro, the veteran PT ideologue, says the right has built up 'the most notable hegemonic apparatus ever constructed by the Brazilian elites' (Genro, 2014). The right-wing agenda which now dominates Congress includes introducing bills that will make it easier for mining companies and agribusiness to evict indigenous communities and peasant families from their land.

In her second term, Dilma, who is not a traditional *petista*, having joined the PT many years after it was founded, has chosen ministers from the centre and right-wing parties, which form part of the ruling coalition. She has done this in the name of governance, but it has led to what appear to many *petistas* as incomprehensible choices, such as the selection of the vociferous anti-MST landowner Kátia Abreu as her Minister of Agriculture, and the climate sceptic Aldo Rebelo as her Minister of Science and Technology. Despite these concessions, there is every indication that relations with Congress will be tempestuous.

The President's inability to choose competent political operators to negotiate with Congress has made things worse. At the beginning of 2015 the National Congress elected a new president who is openly hostile to Dilma, imposing a resounding defeat on her own candidate. Dilma had apparently ignored Lula's advice to avoid such ignominy by negotiating with the eventual winner, Eduardo Cunha, from the PMDB party, a social conservative who is vehemently opposed to the legalization of abortion and wants to create a National Day of Heterosexual Pride. It is an example of the confused state of Brazilian politics that Cunha, who is determined to block the government's agenda at every turn and impose defeats that will seriously compromise the government's budget, belongs to the PMDB, the PT's main partner in the ruling coalition, which provided the vice-president, Michel Temer.

Scandal erupts

In the meantime, the Petrobrás scandal, dubbed *Lava Jato* (Car Wash) by the police, has snowballed. It has been revealed that Petrobrás directors received massive illicit payments from contractors, and then channelled much of it to the PT and its allies in Congress. The sum reported is astronomic: R$2.1 bn (US$650 m, £251 m). The scandal has already led to the sacking of Maria das Graças Foster, a close Dilma aide, as head of

Petrobrás, and to the arrest of the CEOs of several major engineering companies. Since the former head of refining, Paulo Roberto Costa, has turned state witness, more arrests can be expected. Dilma cannot credibly claim that she knew nothing about it: as Minister of Energy during the Lula government, she had a seat on the Petrobrás board when some of the wrongdoing was happening.

Right-wing politicians and the media are determined to pin responsibility exclusively on the PT, although politicians of almost every major party were involved and the scandal began in the PSDB government of Fernando Henrique Cardoso in the 1990s. It is clear that the scandal could checkmate Dilma's government, leaving it paralysed. It has become a justification for right-wing groups to press for the privatization of the giant oil company – something they attempted, and failed to achieve, during the Fernando Henrique Cardoso government.

The more extreme right-wingers are even hoping to use it to unseat the President and have been calling for her impeachment. If the opposition-dominated parliamentary inquiry into the Petrobrás corruption scandal can find evidence which directly implicates her, they would have a case for impeachment. However, many oppositionists seem to prefer a tactic of weakening Dilma's government (some even refer to it as 'bleeding') to such an extent that there is no chance of the PT retaining the presidency at the 2018 elections, even if the candidate were Lula. Whatever happens, the scandal means that Dilma will be permanently on the defensive, fighting off accusations and insinuations. Another area of undoubted tension will be the growing energy and water crisis, as large areas of the south-east grapple with water rationing and water shortages for agriculture.

No reform without mobilization

But the left also has its strengths. Many Brazilians believe that Congress is unfit for purpose and that the country urgently needs wide-ranging political reform. Before the election, in September 2014, over eight million people signed a petition calling for a plebiscite on political reform, including a proposal for a Constituent Assembly and a ban on political parties obtaining electoral campaign funding from private sources. Campaigns would be financed exclusively by a public fund. Miguel Rossetto, who heads the General Secretariat of the Presidency of the Republic, a key position in government, has said that political reform is his priority and that, following Dilma's instructions, he has started negotiations with civil society about how to achieve it (Passos, 2015).

Both the powerful CNBB (*Confederação Nacional dos Bispos do Brasil*, National Confederation of Brazilian Bishops), the Catholic Church's most important body, and the OAB (*Ordem de Advogados Brasileiros*, Brazilian Bar Association), launched a manifesto in February 2015 in which, after saying that the country was living through 'serious political-social difficulties' and that its democratic institutions and electoral process were going through an 'undoubted crisis', they called for political reform (Salamão, 2015).'

In response to the dire political prospects and Dilma's move to the right, social movements are becoming more assertive. One important actor is the MTST, the homeless movement, created in 1997 by Brazil's strong landless movement, the MST, to mobilize around the issue of homelessness in the cities. The MTST has become the largest organization of its kind in Brazil and it achieved an impressive victory in May 2014 when hundreds of families camped in front of the Municipal

Chamber in São Paulo until they achieved the approval by city councillors of a revised and much improved urban planning bill (Sá, 2014). Although the MTST and the MPL are very different, Ortellado says, they are creating closer political links:

> The MTST is an old-style organization with a vertical structure. It has demonstrated brilliantly its capacity for street mobilization without being mixed up in political power. Now the MPL is a different type totally, horizontal, anti-institutional. There have been advances in their capacity to work together (Ortellado, 2014).

The discontent in the country erupted on 15 March when hundreds of thousands of people marched in towns and cities all over Brazil, demanding an end to corruption, especially in Petrobrás. Many of the protesters also called for Dilma's resignation or impeachment. Some even wanted military intervention. Further demonstrations were held in subsequent weeks. Political researcher Bruna Cava says that the new cycle of demonstrations is focusing on corruption for two reasons:

> One is that the issue is in the news every day; and the other – and this is far more real – is because there is a prevalent perception that we are living through the beginning of an economic crisis that the government, distracted by the corruption scandal, is not responding to. On the contrary the government is saying nothing about it. ... So the focussing on corruption ends up, in a certain way, in leading to broader dissatisfaction with the government. And, in a presidential system, this dissatisfaction is centred on the President and in the slogan 'Dilma out'. ... Corruption becomes a way of referring to many other issues. For example,

if someone is unhappy with the health service, with the long queues, and so on, he or she can end up blaming it on corruption. (Cava, 2015)

The scale of the most recent mobilizations has thrown the left, both *petistas* and *non-petistas*, off balance. As Cava points out, the PT encouraged the population to vote for Dilma, talking about the need to protect health, education, labour rights and social welfare. Once elected, however, Dilma moved to implement measures that are closer to those of the programme of the opposition than to that of the PT.

This leaves the left in an uncomfortable and exposed position. Many *petistas* had hoped that the way might be open for another cycle of progressive change. They had calculated that Lula's great and continuing popularity would make him a strong candidate if he were to run in the presidential elections of 2018. With another cycle in government, the PT could move beyond the question of 'social inclusion' – bringing the millions of poor and excluded into Brazilian society as consumers and citizens, a process which is well under way – and move ahead to tackle the more challenging issue of 'social justice'.

In tacit acknowledgement that this was an area where the PT has failed, PT leader Tarso Genro, said soon after Dilmas's re-election in October 2014 that this must now be the party's goal – a radical programme to reduce social inequalities (Genro, 2014). He has also spoken of 'refounding the PT' and moving towards a definitive break with the PMDB (Diário do Centro do Mundo, 2015).

But by April 2015, these optimistic scenarios seemed increasingly unlikely. By then many *petista* activists were in shock and profoundly depressed. Bernardo Kucinski, a renowned journalist and writer, who helped found the PT and worked as a presidential aide in the first Lula administration, believed that, while the impeachment of the President remained unlikely, prospects for the left were dire:

> What is more likely, however, is that Dilma and the PT will be left simmering away under a gentle heat so that all that is left of the PT is completely destroyed and the way is cleared for the advance of the right and the extreme right in next year's municipal elections. Among the right will be new small parties of the extreme right, one of them headed by Bolsonaro [Jair Bolsonaro, a federal deputy] in alliance with the evangelicals. The next step will an overwhelming victory for the right, perhaps hiding behind a PSDB mask, in the 2018 presidential elections (Kucinski, 2015).

Kucinski said that the corruption scandal had taken off in such spectacular fashion because the public had different expectations of the PT: 'The corruption gained a strategic importance because of the barefaced effrontery with which PT leaders and Petrobrás directors adopted the corrupt practices they themselves said they were going to combat. ... Dilma was elected by a party that claimed to be different from the others, to have an ethical code of behaviour.'

The ebbing tide

Historians and activists will speculate for years on what went wrong with the PT experiment but, even at this early stage, some tentative conclusions can be reached. The PT's reforms were piecemeal, not part of a broad attempt to bring about wide-ranging structural change. No attempt was made to change the political system, to challenge the basic tenets of neo-liberalism or to neutralize the hostility of the mainstream media. Such a transformation of Brazilian society would have been difficult, perhaps impossible, but without it the established economic elites remained in place and their power intact. The PT was never really in full control of government but constantly made unsatisfactory, precarious deals with the old guard. As Alfredo Saad-Filho, the Brazilian professor of political economy at SOAS in the University of London, has pointed out, the PT 'accepted a fragile hold on power as a condition of power itself' (Saad-Filho, 2015).

If the party of Lula and Dilma had really intended to create a socially just country, it should have used the enormous groundswell of support its welfare programmes generated among the poor to strengthen social movements and build up an unstoppable momentum for real economic and social change. Instead, it focused far too narrowly on adroit manoeuvring within the current system, in both domestic and foreign policy. So the government used the BNDES to channel huge amounts of money to powerful economic groups to create 'Brazilian champions', without ever thinking how these champions would really benefit the ordinary Brazilian. And with single-minded determination it pushed ahead with the construction of highways and vast hydroelectric dams without considering the environmental and social cost for the country, particularly its poorer citizens.

The PT squandered the chance to reform the educational system and turn it into the means of progressive change, of raising awareness, of building the 'new Brazilian' that the famous anthropologist and educationalist Darcy Ribeiro had envisaged in the 1980s. It also failed, and still fails, to understand the importance of good communications, especially in a country where the mass media is hostile and economical with the truth. The PT made the mistake of thinking that because it believed something was right, everyone would accept it, without the need of explanation or persuasion.

All of which left PT politicians and trade unionists with no option but to play the political game by its old and extremely dirty rules and in doing so they destroyed their 'unique selling point' – their ethical purity. The best that can be hoped for today is that the important social reforms made in the PT's years of government can somehow be salvaged. The challenge of transforming Brazil will be left to a new generation of left-wingers, not associated with the PT, and it may take many years for this to emerge.

The troubles and possible demise of the PT in Brazil come as legitimacy drains away from progressive governments elsewhere in Latin America. Writing in late 2014, the Portuguese sociologist Boaventura de Sousa Santos said (2014):

> Latin America's daring in the last 15 years has been to take advantage of a moment of weakness of hegemonic capitalism. Trapped since the 1990s in the Middle East to satisfy the insatiable military industrial complex and its greed for oil, the USA permitted the advance in its own backyard of forms of nationalism and populism which, differently from the earlier forms, did not target the small urban middle classes but the great mass of excluded and marginalized. They had a strong vocation for social inclusion.

Violent US-sponsored interventions to effect regime change seem unlikely. As Santos notes,

> These today are reserved for small countries like Haiti (2004), Honduras (2009) and Paraguay (2012). But they [the US government] will undertake actions to promote social and political destabilization, they will

encourage popular discontent, finance friendly NGOs and supply technical support for controlling protests and in this way obtain crucial information (ibid.).

Whatever the extent of US intervention, by 2015 the left was suffering setbacks in much of South America, notably in Venezuela, Bolivia and Argentina. In Chile, the exceptionally popular president Michelle Bachelet saw her ratings nosedive when a major corruption scandal implicated her son and she was too slow to respond to the escalating crisis.

If the PT in Brazil loses what remains of its legitimacy, the so-called *onda rosa* or 'pink tide' in Latin America will definitively be on the ebb. None of us can tell when this tide will turn again.

Glossary

Advogados Ativistas Activist Lawyers

Arena Aliança Renovadora Nacional National Renovation Alliance

BNDES Banco Nacional de Desenvolvimento Social e Econômico National Bank of Social and Economic Development

CNBB Conferência Nacional dos Bispos do Brasi National Confederation of Brazilian Bishops

Comitê Popular da Copa Popular Committee for the World Cup

CJP Comissão Justiça e Paz Justice and Peace Commission

CUT Central Única dos Trabalhadores Unified Workers' Council (TUC)

ECLAC Economic Commission for Latin America and the Caribbean

Fórum Brasileiro de Segurança Pública Brazilian Forum for Public Security

FTAA Free Trade Area of the Americas

ICMS Imposto sobre Circulação de Mercadorias e Prestação de Serviços Tax on the Circulation of Goods and Services (VAT)

JR Juventude Revolução Revolutionary Youth

MDB Movimento Democrático Brasileiro Brazilian Democratic Movement

Mercosur Mercado Comum do Sul Common Market of the South

Movimento Xingu Vivo para Sempre Xingu Alive for Ever Movement

MPL Movimento Passe Livre Free Fare Movement
MTST Movimento dos Trabalhadores Sem-Teto
Homeless Workers' Movement
NAFTA North America Free Trade Agreement
OAB Ordem de Advogados Brasileiros Brazilian
Bar Association
PAC 1 Programa de Aceleração do Crescimento 1
Growth Acceleration Programme 1
PAC 2 Programa de Aceleração do Crescimento 2
Growth Acceleration Programme 2
PM Polícia Militar Military Police
PMDB Partido do Movimento Democrático
Brasileiro Brazilian Democratic Movement Party
Pro-Uni Programa Universidade para Todos
University for All Programme
PSB Partido Socialista Brasileiro Brazilian Socialist
Party
PSDB Partido da Social Democracia do Brasil
Social Democratic Party of Brazil
PT Partido dos Trabalhadores Workers' Party
Sindicato de Trabalhadores da Construção
Pesada Union of Workers in Heavy Construction
Unasur União de Nações Sudamericanas Union
of South American Nations

The authors

Sue Branford is a freelance journalist and writer, based in the UK, who used to work for the BBC World Service as a Latin America analyst. The country she knows best in the region is Brazil.

Jan Rocha, based in São Paulo, also freelance, was correspondent for the *Guardian* and the BBC's World Service for many years.

The two were co-authors of *Cutting the Wire: the Story of the Landless Movement in Brazil* (Latin America Bureau, London 2002).

References

All website references were last accessed March 2015, unless otherwise stated

Acary, V. (2014) 'Por que a esquerda socialista terá poucos votos nas eleições de 2014?' *Correio da Cidadania*, 02 September 2014, <http://www.correiocidadania.com.br/index.php?option=com_content&view=article&id=10014:submanchete050914&catid=25:politica&Itemid=47>.

Amnesty International (2013) 'Police still "have blood on their hands" 20 years on from massacre', 24 July 2013, <http://www.amnestyusa.org/news/news-item/brazil-police-still-have-blood-on-their-hands-20-years-after-candelaria-massacre>.

Arraes, V. (2015) 'Estados Unidos e Brasil: aspirações desencontradas no início da gestão de Ibama', *Correio da Cidadania*, 7 April 2015, <http://www.correiocidadania.com.br/index.php?option=com_content&view=article&id=10657:submanchete070415&catid=72:imagens-rolantes>.

Atherton, M. (2014) 'How to back Brazilian regime change', *The Times*, 20 September 2014, <http://www.thetimes.co.uk/tto/money/article4212064.ece>.

Barrucho, L. (2012) 'Brazil strikes headache for President Dilma Rousseff', *BBC World News Latin America* [website], <http://www.bbc.co.uk/news/world-latin-america-19359359> [accessed 14 April 2015].

Benson, T. (2008) 'New fleet may mean U.S. covets Brazil's oil: Lula', *Reuters*, 18 September 2008, <http://www.reuters.com/article/2008/09/18/us-brazil-oil-usa-idUSN1827567620080918> [Accessed 15 April 2015].

Betto, F. (2014) 'Reforma Política Urgente!', *Caros Amigos*, 29 November 2014, <http://www.carosamigos.com.br/index.php/home/historia/247-revista/edicao-214-2/4767-reforma-politica-urgente>.

BNDES (no date) *The Evolution of BNDES' Disbursement*, BNDES, <http://www.bndes.gov.br/SiteBNDES/bndes/bndes_en/Institucional/The_BNDES_in_Numbers/>.

Boadle, A. and Soto, A. (2012) 'Brazil wants to restrict strikes in public sector', *Reuters,* <http://www.reuters.com/article/2012/10/05/brazil-rousseff-strikes-idUSL1E8KQ1CN20121005> [accessed 14 April 2015].

Branford, S. and Kucinski, B. (2003) *Politics transformed: Lula and the Workers' Party in Brazil*, Latin America Bureau, London.

Brant, G. (2004) 'How the U.S. lost Brazil', *Infobrazil*, <http://www.latinamericanstudies.org/brazil/lost.htm>.

Brito, G. (2014) 'O poder judiciário está se submetendo às decisões do executivo e a repressão tende a aumentar', *Correio da Cidadania*, 1 August 2014, <http://www.correiocidadania.com.br/index.php?option=com_content&task=view&id=9891>.

Brum, E. (2013) 'Dois Josés e um Amarildo', *El País*, 26 November 2013, <http://brasil.elpais.com/brasil/2013/11/25/opinion/1385417332_769557.html>.

Carter M. (ed.) (2015) *Challenging Social Inequality: The Landless Rural Workers Movement and Agrarian Reform in Brazil*, Durham, NC: Duke University Press.

Caulyt, F. (2014) 'Cuban doctor in Brazil triggers diplomatic tiff', *Deutsche Welle*, 13 February 2014, <http://www.dw.de/cuban-doctor-in-brazil-triggers-diplomatic-tiff/a-17428537>.

Cava, N. (2015), 'A esquerda desconectada e o impasse das novas manifestações. Entrevista especial com Bruno Cava', Instituto Humanitas Unisinos, 16 April 2015, <http://www.ihu.unisinos.br/entrevistas/541815-a-esquerda-desconectada-e-o-impasse-das-novas-manifestacoes-entrevista-especial-com-bruno-cava>.

CIA (2014) *The World Fact Book 2014*, <http://tinyurl.com/q8xo9qd>.

Costa, I. Junior (2014) 'Brasil piorou em educação e segurança pública e a economia não cresceu. Dá para melhorar em 2014?', *Jornal Opção*, Contraponto, 5–11 January 2014, <http://www.jornalopcao.com.br/colunas/contraponto/brasil-piorou-em-educacao-e-seguranca-publica-e-a-economia-nao-cresceu.-da-para-melhorar-em-2014>.

Diário do Centro do Mundo (2015) 'Tarso Genro defende guinada à esquerda do PT', 28 December 2015, <http://www.diariodocentrodomundo.com.br/essencial/tarso-genro-defende-guinada-a-esquerda-do-pt/>.

Fachin, P. et al. (2011) 'Belo Monte: Coerção nos canteiros de obra. Entrevista especial com Ruy Sposato', *IHU Online*, Nova Sindical de Trabalhadores do Paraná, 5 December 2011, <http://www.ncstpr.org.br/index.php?option=com_content&view=article&id=4224:belo-monte-coercao-nos-canteiros-de-obra-entrevista-especial-com-ruy-sposato&catid=33:ultimas-noticias&Itemid=168>, [accessed 14 April 2015].

Fakier, K. and Ehmke, E. (2014) *Socio-Economic Insecurity in Emerging Economies*, Google eBook <http://books.google.co.uk/books?id=Xq3AAwAAQBAJ&dq=Brazil+trade+unions+and+pension+funds>.

Fitzpatrick, M.J. (2011) 'Conference: A Southern Cone Perspective on Chavez's Influence', published from Wikileaks, *Pagina/12*, 7 March 2011, Buenos Aires, <http://www.pagina12.com.ar/diario/elpais/sub-notas/163623-52406-2011-03-07.html> [accessed 1 April 2015]

Fox, M. (2010) 'After Lula: Brazil's foreign policy at a Crossroad', *New America Media*, 29 November 2010,

<http://newamericamedia.org/2010/11/after-lula-brazils-foreign-policy-at-a-crossroads.php>.

Genro, T. (2014) 'Frente de esquerda na diversidade da esquerda', *Carta Maior*, 27 December 2014, <http://cartamaior.com.br/?/Editoria/Politica/Fr-de-esquerda-na-diversidade-da-esquerda/4/32526>.

Hunt, D. (2015) 'PMDB: Brazil's invisible government', *Brasil Wire*, 01 March 2015, <http://www.brasilwire.com/pmdb-brasils-invisible-government/>.

IHU Online (2011), 'A 'moderna' indústria brasileira de carne. Produçãa a custa da saúde e da vida dos trabalhadores', *IHU* Online, 23 September 2011, <http://www.ihu.unisinos.br/entrevistas/500466-a-moderna-industria-brasileira-da-carne-producao-a-custa-da-saude-e-da-vida-dos-trabalhadores-entrevista-especial-com-siderlei-de-oliveira>, [accessed 14 April 2015].

Kucinski, B. (2015) 'Brazil – the death of the PT', *LAB*, 1 April 2015, <http://lab.org.uk/brazil-the-death-of-the-pt>.

Leahy, J. (2015) 'BNDES: lender of first resort for Brazil's tycoons', *Financial Times*, 11 January 2015, <http://www.ft.com/cms/s/0/c510368e-968e-11e4-922f-00144feabdc0.html#axzz3RcWEMTlO>.

Lima, N. (2014) 'Tucanos, a Alca e a Petrobrás', *Petroleiroanistiado* [blog], <https://petroleiroanistiado.wordpress.com/2014/04/24/tucanos-a-alca-e-a-petrobras/>.

Loman, H. et al. (2014) 'Brazil's Social Challenges', *Economic Report*, Rabobank, <https://economics.rabobank.com/publications/2014/january/brazils-social-challenges>.

Machado, U. (2011) 'Entrevista Jessé Souza', in *A Folha de S. Paulo*, 13 February 2011, <http://www1.folha.uol.com.br/fsp/poder/po1302201106.htm>.

National Coalition (2012) (National Coalition of Local Committees for a People's World Cup and Olympics) *Megaevents and Human Rights Violations in Brazil*, June 2012, <http://rioonwatch.org/wp-content/uploads/2013/05/2012-World-Cup-Olympics-Dossier-English.pdf>.

Neri, M. (2012) (coordinator), *Back to the Country of the Future: Forecasts, European Crisis and the New Middle Class in Brazil*, Fundação Getúlio Vargas (FGV), Rio de Janeiro, <http://www.cps.fgv.br/cps/bd/ncm2014/NCM2014_ENG_SUMARIO_final.pdf>.

Ortellado, P. (2014) interviewed by Coletivo Copa, 'Sempre que houver a menor ameaça de mobilização social, teremos suspensão de direitos básicos', *Correio da Cidadania*, 23 July 2014, <http://www.correiocidadania.com.br/index.php?option=com_content&task=view&id=9855&Itemid=79> [Accessed 15 April 2015].

Passos, N. (2015) 'Reforma Política é compromisso prioritário, diz Miguel Rossetto', *Carta Maior*, 13 January 2015, <http://cartamaior.com.br/?/Editoria/Politica/Reforma-politica-e-compromisso-prioritario-diz-Miguel-Rosseto/4/32623>.

Pomar, M. (2013) interviewed by Coletivo Maria Tonha, 'Ele ajudou a fundar o Movimento Passe Livre', *Tarifa Zero*, 25 July 2013, <http://tarifazero.org/2013/07/25/ele-ajudou-a-fundar-o-movimento-passe-livre-entrevista-com-marcelo-pomar/>, [accessed 15 April 2015].

Pomar, W. (2014) 'Questões do desenvolvimento brasileiro', *Correio da Cidadania*, 6 August 2014, <http://www.correiocidadania.com.br/index.php?option=com_content&view=article&id=9915:pomar070814&catid=14:wladimir-pomar&Itemid=88>.

Romero, S. (2015) '"Bullet caucus" in Brazil signals political shift to the left', *New York Times*, 14 January 2015 <http://www.nytimes.com/2015/01/15/world/americas/bullet-caucus-in-brazil-signals-a-shift-to-the-right.html?_r=2>.

Sá, E. (2014) 'Novo Plano Diretor é aprovado em São Paulo com pressão dos Sem Teto (SP)', *Pela Moradia*, <https://pelamoradia.wordpress.com/2014/07/11/novo-plano-diretor-e-aprovado-em-sao-paulo-com-pressao-dos-sem-teto-sp/>.

Saad-Filho, A. (2015) 'Brazil: the Débâcle of the PT', *Socialist Project*, E-Bulletin No. 1097, 30 March 2015, <http://www.socialistproject.ca/bullet/1097.php>.

Salamão, L. (2015) 'CNBBB e AOB lançam manifesto de apoio à reforma política', *globo.com*, 25 February 2015, <http://g1.globo.com/politica/noticia/2015/02/cnbb-e-oab-lancam-manifesto-de-apoio-reforma-politica.html>.

Santos, B. (2014) 'Brasil: a grande divisão', *Carta Maior*, 18 November 2014, <http://cartamaior.com.br/?/Editoria/Politica/Brasil-a-grande-divisao/4/32259>.

Senra, R. (2014) 'SalaSocial: Sem-teto, índios e LGBT moldam crítica de esquerda ao PT', *BBC Brasil*, http://www.bbc.co.uk/portuguese/noticias/2014/11/141107_salasocial_votocritico_rs.

Soares, S. (2012) 'Bolsa Família: a summary of its impacts', *International Policy Centre for Inclusive Growth*, Institute for Applied Economic Research (IPEA), <http://www.ipc-undp.org/pub/IPCOnePager137.pdf>.

Souza, J. (2009) 'A Ralé Brasileira: Quem é e Como Vive', Universidade Federal de Minas Gerais, pp. 15-71, Belo Horizonte.

Stewart, J.B. (2014) 'In Brazil's Election, a Stark Vote on the Nation's Economy', *The New York Times*, 24 October 2014, <http://www.nytimes.com/2014/10/25/business/in-brazil-election-a-stark-choice-on-economic-direction.html>.

Studart, R. (2013) 'Lessons from Brazil to get rid of poverty', *The Economic Times*, 26 March 2013, <http://articles.economictimes.indiatimes.com/2013-03-26/news/38040303_1_extreme-poverty-poverty-line-bolsa-familia>.

The Economist (2014) 'Why Brazil needs change', *The Economist*, 18 October 2014, <http://www.economist.com/news/leaders/21625780-voters-should-ditch-dilma-rousseff-and-elect-cio-neves-why-brazil-needs-change>.

Yang, S. (2015) 'Eike Batista is now a "negative billion-aire"', Yahoo Finance, 13 Feb 2015, <http://finance.yahoo.com/news/eike-batista-now-negative-billion-aire-163310541.html>

Zibechi, R. (2014) The New Brazil – Regional Imperial-ism and the New Democracy, Edinburgh: AK Press.

Latin America Bureau (LAB)

LAB is an independent charitable organization, based in London, which provides news, analysis and information on Latin America, reporting consistently from the perspective of the region's poor, oppressed or marginalized communities and social movements. LAB brings an alternative, critical awareness and understanding of Latin America to readers throughout the English-speaking world.

LAB is widely known for its books and operates a website, updated daily, in which it carries news and analysis on Latin America and reports from our partners and correspondents in the region (www.lab.org.uk).

CPSIA information can be obtained
at www.ICGtesting.com
Printed in the USA
FFOW01n0942120216
21385FF

9 781909 014015